Science 1

for Christian Schools®

BJU PRESS

GREENVILLE, SOUTH CAROLINA

dis•cern•ment
(dĭ-sûrn'mənt)

n. 1. Clear, accurate perception. 2. Sound judgment and keen insight.

The fact that your student has this BJU Press product is evidence that you have exercised not only discernment in your choice of the finest state-of-the-art materials available, but you have also exercised trust—something we remember here every single day. You will not regret choosing a BJU Press Science textbook.

- **Enjoy** interacting with your student to discover the amazing secrets of God's world through daily activities that go beyond reading and include doing.

- **Relax** at test time— your student will be ready and the test prepared for you.

- **Watch** the subject take hold of your student as the process of learning for life begins.

Science 1

for Christian Schools®

Second Edition

Candace J. Levesque

This textbook was written by members of the faculty and staff of Bob Jones University. Standing for the "old-time-religion" and the absolute authority of the Bible since 1927, Bob Jones University is the world's leading Fundamentalist Christian university. The staff of the University is devoted to educating Christian men and women to be servants of Jesus Christ in all walks of life.

Providing unparalleled academic excellence, Bob Jones University prepares its students through its offering of over one hundred majors, while its fervent spiritual emphasis prepares their minds and hearts for service and devotion to the Lord Jesus Christ.

If you would like more information about the spiritual and academic opportunities available at Bob Jones University, please call *1-800-BJ-AND-ME* (1-800-252-6363).
www.bju.edu

SCIENCE 1 for Christian Schools®
Second Edition

Candace J. Levesque

Design	Composition	Project Coordinator
John Bjerk	Kelley Moore	Vic Ludlum
Elly Kalagayan		
Joel Leineweber		
Wendy Searles		

Produced in cooperation with the Bob Jones University Department of Science Education of the School of Education, the College of Arts and Science, and Bob Jones Elementary School.

Photo credits appear on pages 166-67.

for Christian Schools is a registered trademark of BJU Press.

© 1989, 1998, 2003 BJU Press
Greenville, South Carolina 29614
First Edition © 1975 BJU Press

Printed in the United States of America
All rights reserved

ISBN 1-57924-908-6

15 14 13 12 11 10 9 8 7 6 5 4 3 2 1

Contents

Your Senses

CHAPTER ONE

God gave you five senses.
You see, touch, taste, smell, and hear.
You find out science with your senses.
You are a scientist!

Seeing

"He that formed the eye, shall he not see?" Psalm 94:9

You see big things and little things.
You see long things and short things.
You see thick things and thin things.
You see many different sizes.

4

You see things shaped like circles and squares.
You see things shaped like triangles and rectangles.
You see many different shapes.

You see red things and blue things.
You see yellow things and purple things.
You see orange things and green things.
You see many different colors.

Touching

"And [they] besought him that they might only touch the hem of his garment: and as many as touched were made perfectly whole." Matthew 14:36

Touch your desk. Is it hard or soft?
Touch your book. Is it rough or smooth?
Touch your face. Is it hot or cold?

You touch many different textures.
You touch many different temperatures.

Tasting

"How sweet are thy words unto my taste! yea, sweeter than honey to my mouth!" Psalm 119:103

Do you think lemons taste sweet or sour?
Do you think pretzels taste salty or bitter?
You taste many different flavors.

8

Finding Out... by Tasting

1. Get

some different flavors to taste   some cups   some cotton swabs

2. Pinch your nose shut.

3. Taste what is in cup 1.
   What flavor did you taste?

4. Record what you observed.

5. Test the flavors in the other cups.

Smelling

You smell strawberries, baking bread,
and twisty, black licorice.
You smell rotten eggs, dirty socks,
and old, sweaty sneakers.
You smell many different odors.

Hearing

"Speak, Lord; for thy servant heareth." I Samuel 3:9

You hear snap, crackle, and pop.
You hear fizz, rattle, and clank.
You hear many different sounds.

12

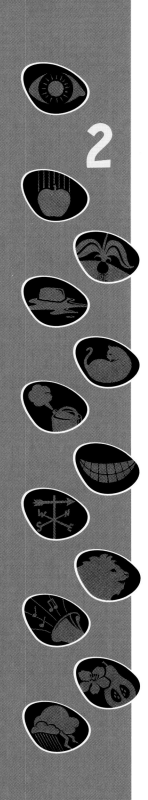

2

Sun, Moon, and Stars

The Sun

"And God made . . . the greater light to rule the day."
Genesis 1:16

You see the sun in the sky.
The sun is a star.
It is the closest star to Earth.

The sun has different parts.
One part of the sun is the surface.
It is the round, yellow part you see every day.

Another part of the sun is the crown.
It is the glowing, white part
that scientists see only at special times.
The crown of the sun is heat and light
coming from the surface of the sun.

The sun has a special path.

In the morning
the sun is in the east.

At noon
the sun is overhead.

In the evening
the sun is in the west.

17

Finding Out... About the Sun

1. Get

   two cards   a pencil

2. Write an *E* on one card and a *W* on the other card.

3. Put the *E* card where the sun comes up, and the *W* card where the sun goes down.

4. Turn so your left hand points to the *E* card.

5. Make your fingertips touch over your head to show the sun's path.

6. Record what you did.

The Moon

"And God made . . . the lesser light to rule the night."
Genesis 1:16

You see the moon in the sky.
The moon is a big ball made of rock.
It is closer to Earth than the sun is.

The moon has big dark places on it. Some people think the dark places look like a man. What do you think they look like?

The moon seems to change shape.
Which shapes have you seen?

20

The Stars

"And God made . . . the stars also." Genesis 1:16

You see the stars in the sky.
You see the closest star only in the day.
That star is the sun.
You see the other stars only at night.

Stars seem to form pictures in the sky.
Can you find a dipper
in this group of stars?

Can you find a great hunter
in this group of stars?

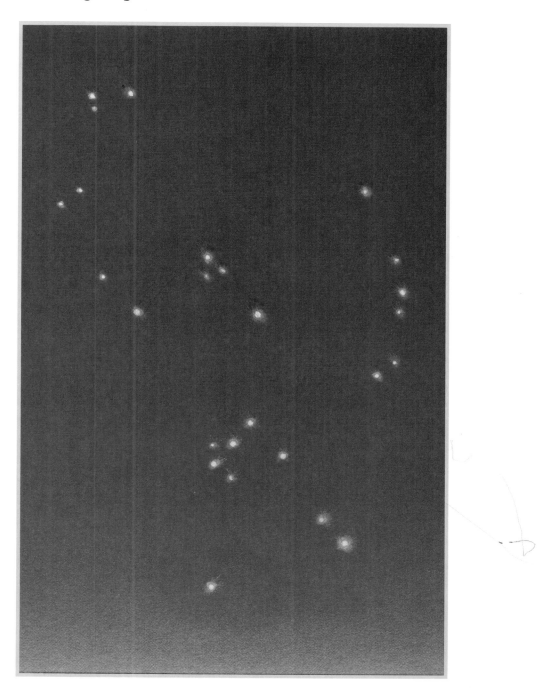

Look at the picture.
What makes stars seem to twinkle?

"Ah Lord God! behold, thou hast made
the heaven and the earth by thy great power
and stretched out arm, and there is nothing too
hard for thee."   *Jeremiah 32:17*

3

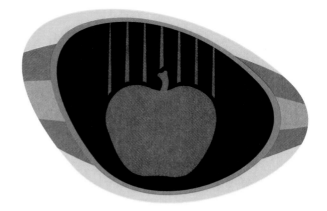

Pushes
and Pulls

A force is a push or a pull.
God made different kinds of forces.

Gravity

The earth and the moon cause a force.
This force is gravity.

What does gravity do?

Gravity makes
many things
come down.

Magnetic Force

Magnets cause a force.
This is magnetic force.

What does magnetic force do?
Magnetic force holds some
things together.

Finding Out...

About Magnetic Force

1. Get

a magnet   some things to test

2. Bring your magnet close to one thing.

3. Observe what happens.
   Does the magnet stick to the thing?

4. Record what you observed.

5. Test the other things.

Mechanical Force

People, animals, and machines cause a force.
The locomotive is causing a force
on the cars of the train.
The tractor is causing a force on the plow.
This is mechanical force.

What does
mechanical
force do?

Mechanical force starts movement.
It also stops movement.

The boy kicks the ball.
The ball starts moving.

The dog is running away.
The girl tugs the leash
and the dog stops.

Friction

The boy is causing a force on the box.
This is mechanical force.
But what else is causing a force on the box?
The carpet is causing a force on the box.
This force is friction.

What does friction do?

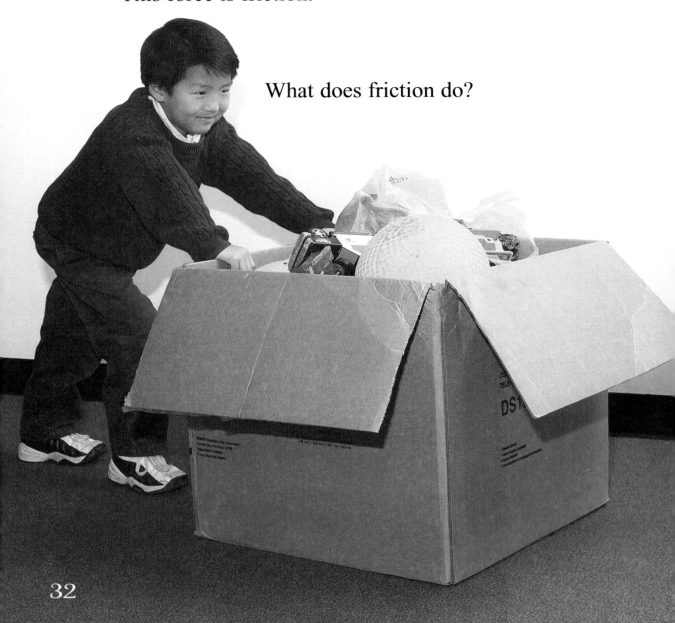

Friction works against movement.
Sometimes you want friction.

Friction keeps your feet
from sliding on the ground.
So it helps you walk and run.
It helps you
stop too.

But if there isn't enough friction,
you can increase it.

To make more friction, you make surfaces rougher. Tread makes surfaces of tires and sneakers rougher. Chains make surfaces of tires rougher too.

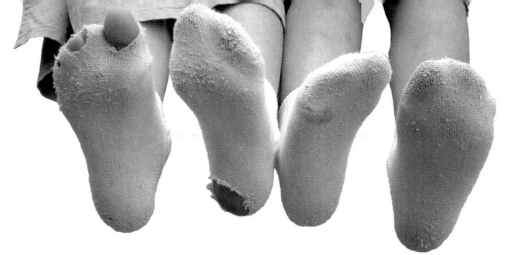

Remember, friction works against movement.
Sometimes you don't want friction.

What made the socks change?
What made the drawer stick?

Friction makes things wear out.
Friction makes things stick.

If there is too much friction,
you can decrease it.

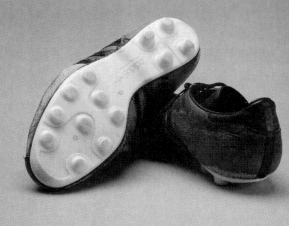

To make less friction,
you make surfaces smoother.

What is making the parts
in the machine smoother?
Which shoe will work better
for ice skating? Why?

*"Great things doeth he, which we
cannot comprehend." Job 37:5*

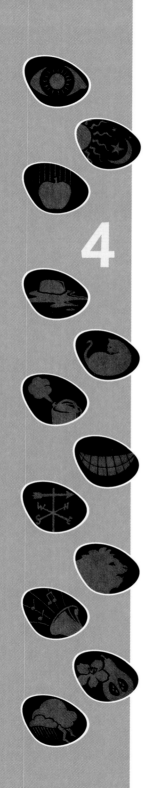

4

Roots, Stems, and Leaves

CHAPTER FOUR

Parts for Growing

Many plants have three parts for growing.
They have roots.
They have stems.
They have leaves.

Leaves

Stem

Roots

Look at the special drawing of this garden.
Find the three parts of each plant.

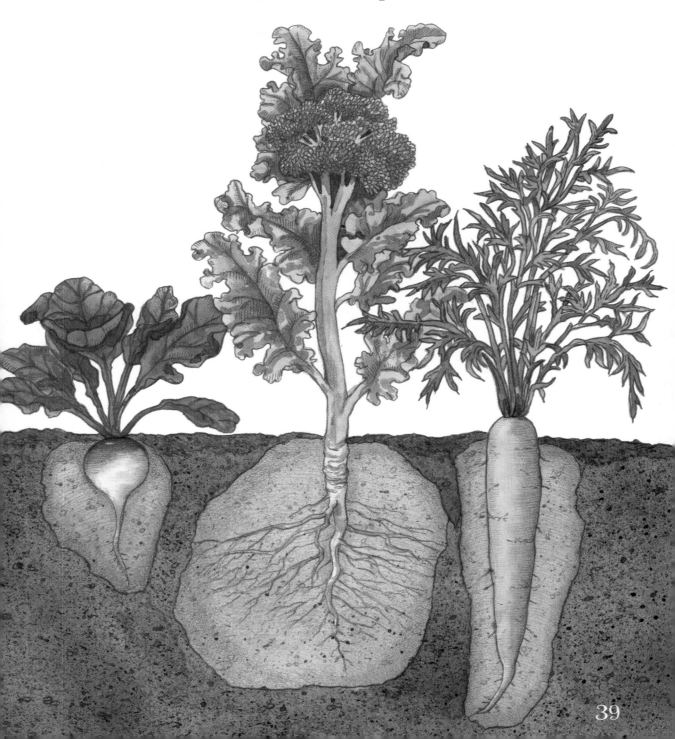

How do roots, stems, and leaves
help plants grow?

Roots take in water for the plant.
Leaves make food for the plant.
Stems carry water from the roots to the leaves.
They also carry food from the leaves
to the roots.

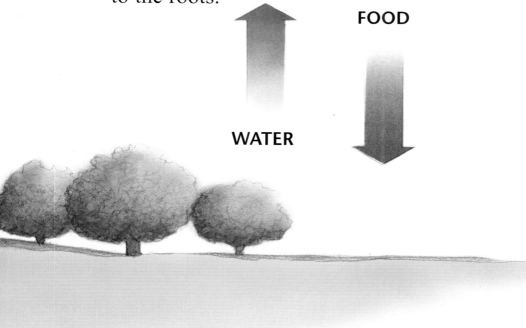

FOOD

WATER

Parts for Grouping

Plants can be put into groups by kinds of
roots, stems, or leaves.

Many plants have one thick root.
Others have many thin ones.

Find the plants with those kinds of roots.

Many plants have
smooth stems.
Others have rough stems.

Find the plants with those
kinds of stems.

Many plants have wide, flat leaves.
Others have leaves that are long and very thin.

Find the plants with those kinds of leaves.

*"Blessed is the man that trusteth in the Lord. . . .
For he shall be as a tree planted by the waters,
. . . and shall not see when heat cometh, but her leaf
shall be green." Jeremiah 17:7-8*

44

About Leaves

1. Get

some leaves

2. Place the leaves in groups by shape.
   Did you get two groups?

3. Record what you observed.

45

Parts for Eating

Plant parts can be food.
Roots can be food.
Stems and leaves can be
food too.

Look at the pictures.
Find the pictures of roots
that people eat.
Find the pictures of stems
and the pictures of leaves.

About Plants People Eat

1. Get

some plants people eat

2. Decide which part you could eat.

3. Record what you did.

leaves

roots

What Is Matter?

CHAPTER FIVE

Matter Takes Up Space

"The works of the Lord are great." Psalm 111:2

Look at the picture of this room.
The stuff takes up a lot of space.
Everything that takes up space is called matter.

You can see paintbrushes and paint. Both the paintbrushes and the paint take up space.

You cannot see the air in the room. But it takes up space.

Even air is matter.

Matter Can Be Weighed

All matter takes up space.
It also can be weighed.
The glass can be weighed.
The milk can be weighed.

The balloon can be weighed.
The air inside the balloon
can be weighed.
All matter can be weighed.

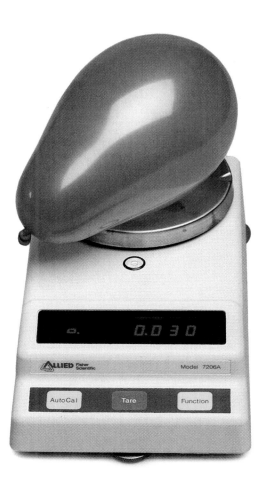

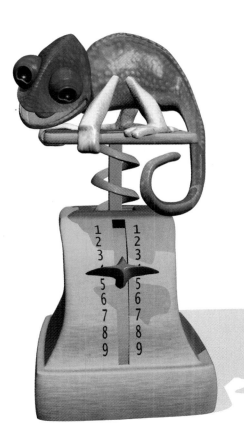

1. Get

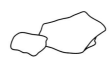

a glass of water   a rock   a small bottle of glue

a flashlight   some masking tape   a scale

2. Put a piece of tape on the glass
   to show the height of the water.

3. Talk into the water.
   Did the level of the
   water go up?
   Does sound take up space?

4. Record what you observed.

5. Test the rock, the bottle of glue, and the light from the flashlight.

6. Talk onto the scale.
   Did the scale move?
   Can sound be weighed?

7. Record what you observed.

8. Test the rock, the bottle of glue, and the light from the flashlight.

Matter Can Be Found in Three Forms

God created three forms of matter.
One form of matter is solid.
Liquid is another form of matter.
Gas is a form of matter too.

Matter in the Solid Form

Look at the pictures.
Do solids change size?
Do solids change shape?

56

Solids do not change size.
They can't get smaller and smaller and smaller.
They can't get bigger and bigger either.

Solids do not change shape.
Your book can't wind itself
around your fingers.

Look at the pictures.
Do liquids change size?
Do liquids change shape?

Liquids do not change size.
They can't get bigger and bigger and bigger.
They can't get smaller and smaller either.

But liquids do change shape.
They will change to the shape
of their containers.

Milk can take the shape of a bottle, a glass, or a bowl.

Matter in the Gas Form

Gases change size.
They can get bigger and bigger.
They can get as big as their containers.

Look at the pictures of the different containers.
There is a gas in each one.
Do gases change shape?

60

Gases change shape.
They will take the shape of their containers.

61

Finding Out...

About Solids, Liquids, and Gases

1. Get

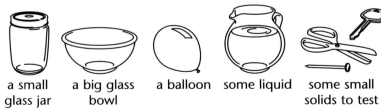

a small glass jar   a big glass bowl   a balloon   some liquid   some small solids to test

2. Put each solid into the bowl.
   Did any of the solids change shape?

3. Pour the liquid into the bowl.
   Did the liquid change shape?

4. Hold the small jar so it fills with liquid.

5. Put gas from the balloon
   into the jar full of liquid.
   Did the gas change shape?

6. Record what you observed.

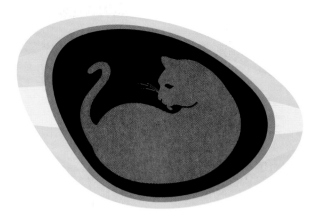

Tame Animals

Some animals are tame.
Tame animals live with people.

*"A righteous man regardeth the
life of his beast."*

Proverbs 12:10

64

Tame Animals in Homes

Pets are tame animals that live in homes.

Dogs, cats, and birds are some pets.

What other animals do people keep as pets?

Do you have a pet?
What is it?

65

What do pets do for people?
Some sing.
Some play.
Some help their owners.

What do you do for a pet?
You give it food.
You give it water.
You give it a place to live and sleep.

Tame Animals on Farms

Livestock are tame animals
that are raised on farms.
Sheep, pigs, and cows are kinds of livestock.

What other animals do people keep as livestock?
Do you keep livestock? What do you keep?

How do livestock help you?
Some give you clothes.
Some give you food.
Some give you work.

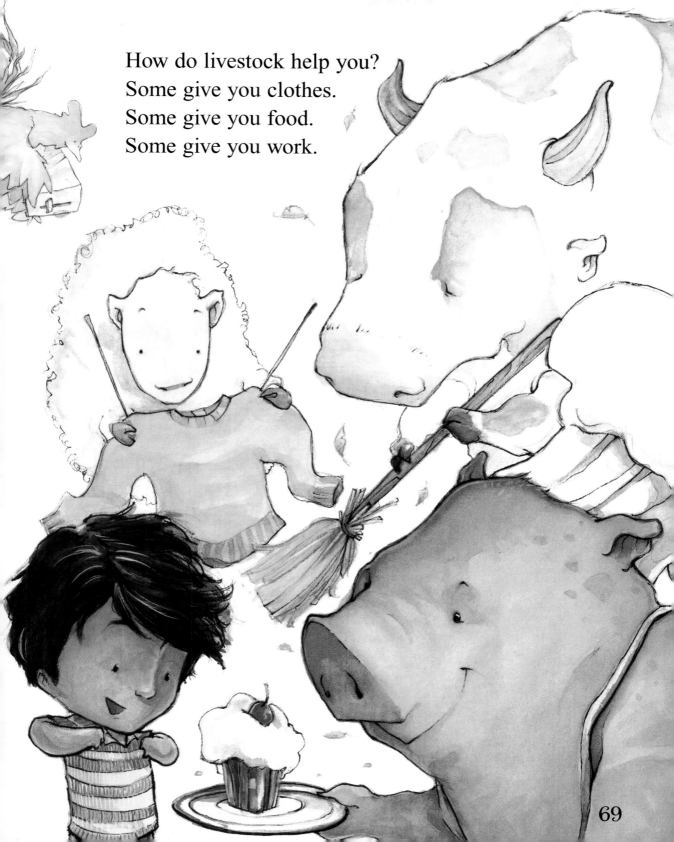

What does a farmer do for his livestock?
He gives them food.
He gives them water.
He gives them a place to live.

"*The Lord is my shepherd . . .*
He maketh me to lie down in green pastures:
he leadeth me beside the still waters.
. . . I will dwell in the house of the Lord
for ever." Psalm 23

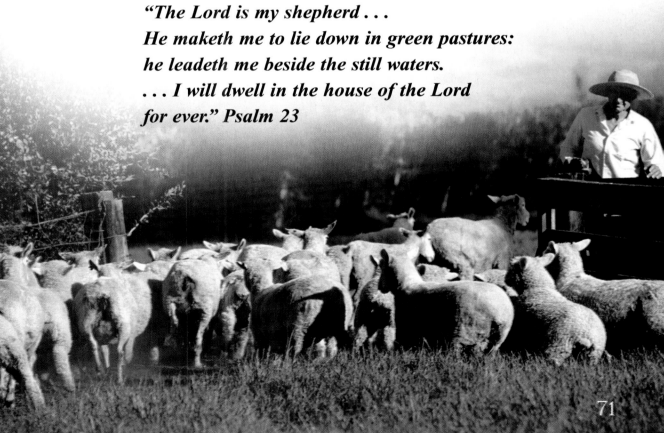

About Livestock

1. Get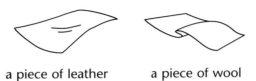

a piece of leather   a piece of wool

2. Feel the leather and the wool.

3. Decide which animal each one came from.

4. Record what you did.

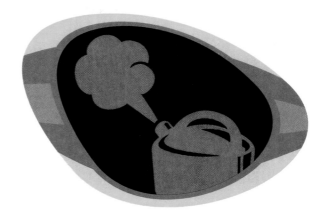

What Can Heat Do?

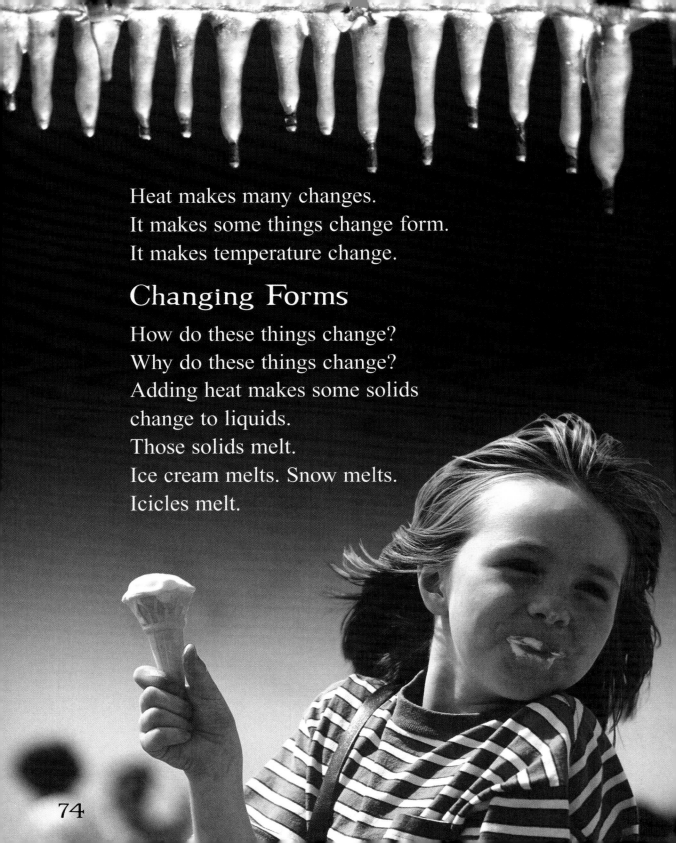

Heat makes many changes.
It makes some things change form.
It makes temperature change.

Changing Forms

How do these things change?
Why do these things change?
Adding heat makes some solids
change to liquids.
Those solids melt.
Ice cream melts. Snow melts.
Icicles melt.

How do these things change?
Why do these things change?

Taking away heat
makes some liquids change to solids.
Those liquids freeze.
Juice freezes. Water freezes. Milk freezes.

Where does the water go?
Adding heat makes some liquids vaporize.
They change to gases.
The gases go into the air.
You cannot see them.

What makes the drops on
the glass?
What makes the drops on
the window?
Taking away heat makes
some gases condense.
They change back to liquids.
You cannot see the gases.
But you can see the liquids.

Changing Temperature

Adding heat makes temperature go up.
Taking heat away makes temperature go down.

How do you know heat changes temperature?

Hot   Warm

You can feel temperature changes.
And you can tell about the changes you feel.
You use words like *hot* and *warm*.
You use words like *cool* and *cold*.

Cool

Cold

How can you show that heat changes temperature?
You can use a thermometer.
Numbers on a thermometer
tell about temperature.
Numbers at the top
tell about hot or warm things.
Numbers at the bottom
tell about cool or cold things.
Look at these pairs of thermometers.
Where is the liquid in each one?
Did the temperature go up or down?
Does that mean heat was added or taken away?

"For I am the Lord,
I change not."
Malachi 3:6

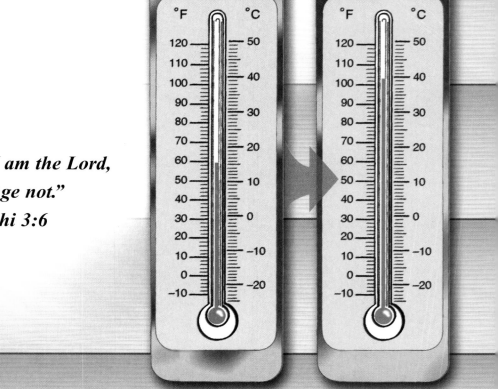

81

About Temperature

1. Get

a thermometer

2. Look at the liquid.
   Where is the liquid?

3. Record what you observed.

4. Hold the liquid end of the thermometer in your hand.

5. Look at the liquid again.
   Where is the liquid?
   Was heat added or taken away?

6. Record what you observed.

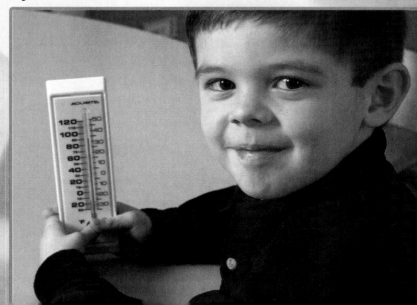

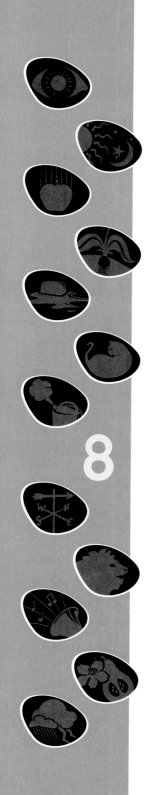

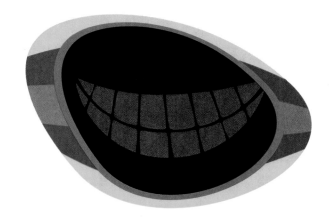

Your Teeth

The Design of Teeth

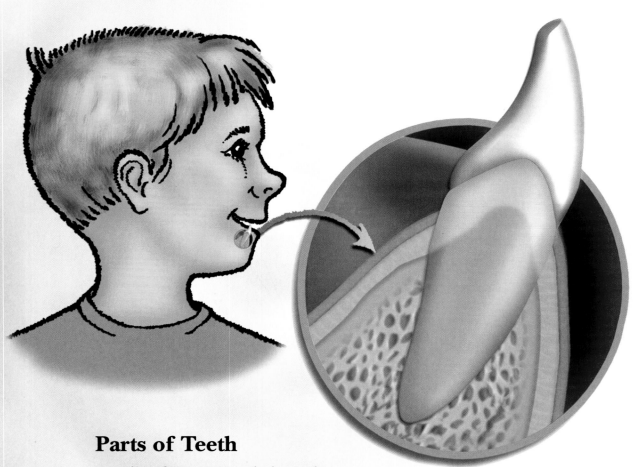

Parts of Teeth

Each of your teeth has three parts.
The crown is the part at the top.
The neck is the part in the gums.
The root is the part in the bone.

Sets of Teeth

Each of your teeth belongs to a set.
God gave you two different sets.

How are these sets different?

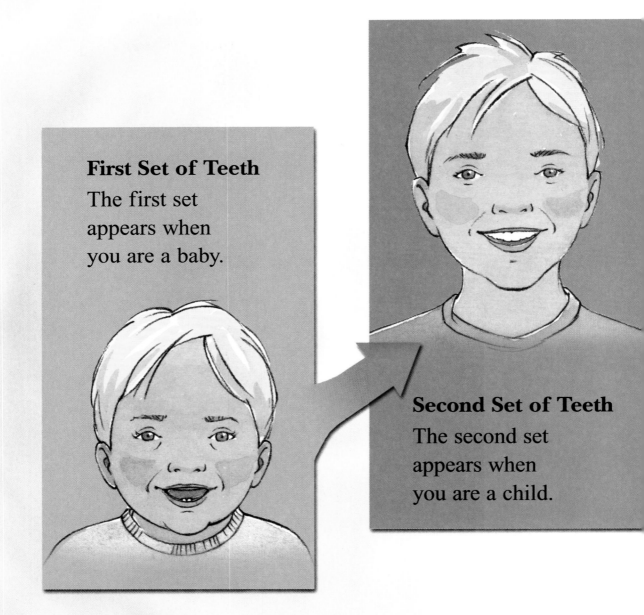

First Set of Teeth
The first set appears when you are a baby.

Second Set of Teeth
The second set appears when you are a child.

First Set of Teeth
The first set has
fewer teeth.
It has smaller teeth.
The first set falls out.

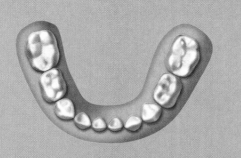

Second Set of Teeth
The second set
has more teeth.
It has larger teeth.

The second set
should not fall out.

Why are these sets different?

"And the Lord said unto him, Who hath made man's mouth? . . . have not I the Lord?"

Exodus 4:11

You can see God's plan
in the way your teeth look.

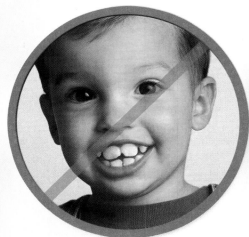

Small mouths need small teeth.

Large mouths need large teeth.

You can see God's plan
in the way your teeth grow.

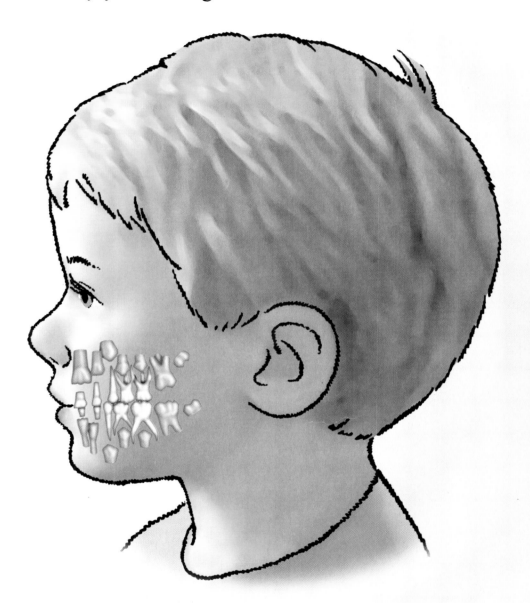

Shapes of Teeth

Each of your teeth has a certain shape.
Some are sharp. Some are pointed.   Some are bumpy.

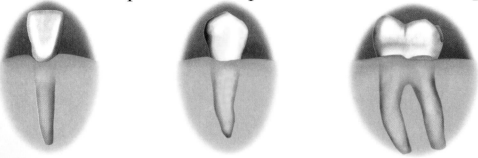

Feel your teeth.
Can you find each shape?

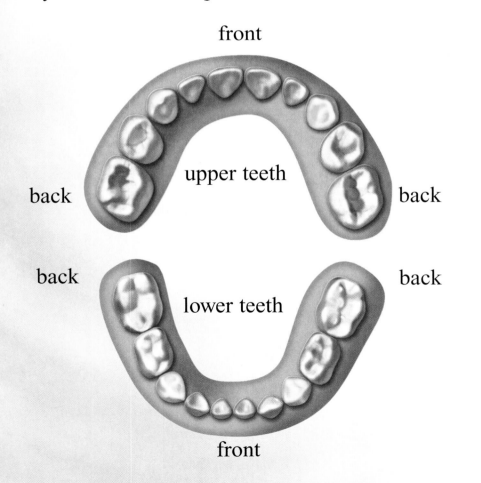

front

upper teeth

back

back

back

back

lower teeth

front

Jobs of Teeth

You use your teeth to chew food.
Animals do too.
Which teeth do you use for each different job?

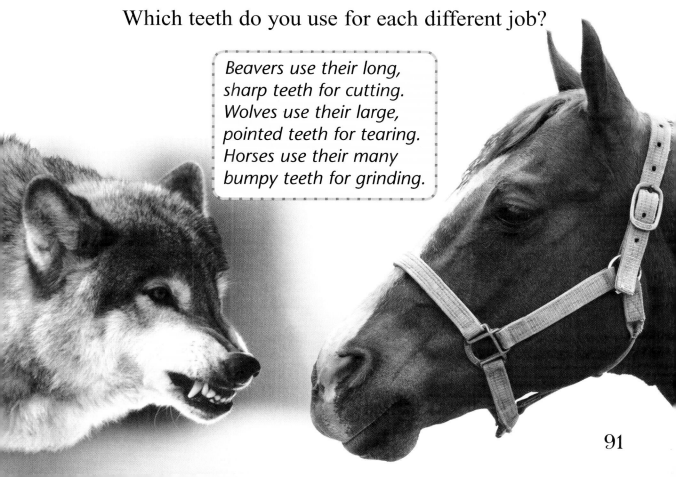

Beavers use their long, sharp teeth for cutting. Wolves use their large, pointed teeth for tearing. Horses use their many bumpy teeth for grinding.

91

Finding Out...

How Your Teeth Work

1. Get

a cracker

a stick of celery

2. Bite off a piece of cracker and chew it. Which teeth did you use to bite the cracker? Which teeth did you use to chew the cracker?

3. Use your teeth to tear off a piece of celery. Which teeth did you use?

4. Record what you observed.

You also use your teeth in other ways.
You use your teeth to help you speak.

Describe the pictures on this page.
Listen carefully to the words you use.
Which sounds did your teeth help you make?

vase

fox

feather

moth

The Care of Teeth

God gave you strong, healthy teeth.
It is your job to take care of them.
How can you take care of your teeth?

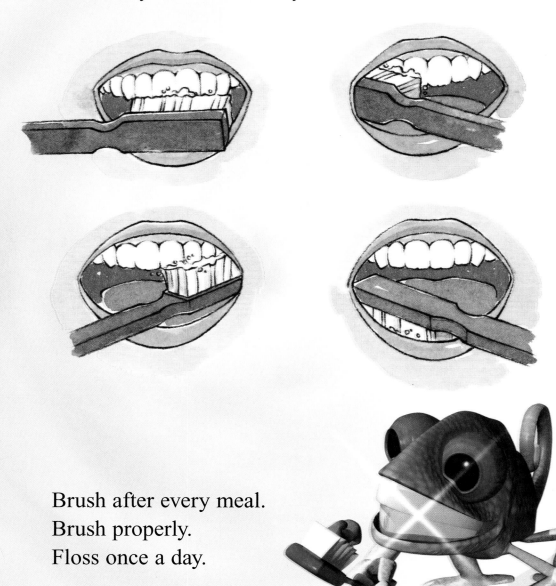

Brush after every meal.
Brush properly.
Floss once a day.

Good Food

Choose snacks that are good
for your teeth. Use fluoride.

Visit the dentist often.

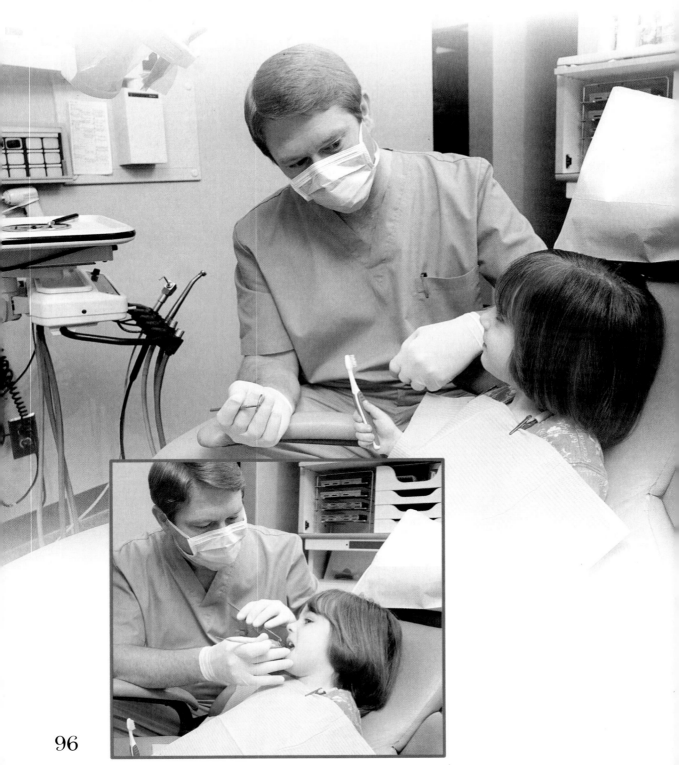

9

What Is
Air Like?

What is the air like in your town today?

Is it hot or cold?
Is it moving or still?
Is it wet or dry?
Weather is the way the air is
at a certain time
in a certain place.

In this chapter you will learn
what causes weather.

The Temperature of Air

Study the pictures.
Tell how you think air gets warm.

The sun gives heat to land and water.
They get warm.
Land and water give heat to air.
It gets warm.

The Movement of Air

Wind is moving air.
A fan moves air.
Heat moves air too.

Remember, land and
water give heat to air.
And air gets warm.
When air gets warm,
it rises.

Why do the horses go
around when the
candles are burning?

Warm air rises higher and higher.
Soon it gets cool.
When air gets cool, it settles.

Where will the girl feel the cool air?

Finding Out... **About Wind**

1. Get

a small lamp

a tray of ice cubes

2. Hold one hand over the lamp and one under it.
   Is the warm air rising or settling?

3. Hold one hand over the ice cube tray and one under it.
   Is the cool air rising or settling?

4. Record what you observed.

The Water in Air

"Seek him . . . that calleth for the waters of the sea, and poureth them out upon the face of the earth: The Lord is his name." Amos 5:8

Water does three things over and over.

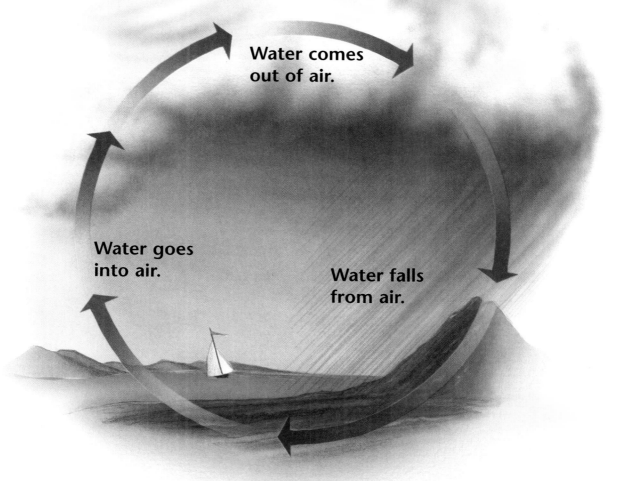

Water comes out of air.

Water goes into air.

Water falls from air.

This is the water cycle.

You will study each part of the water cycle.

Water Goes into Air

Remember, the sun gives heat
to land and water.
Water is a liquid.
When the sun gives heat to water,
water changes to water vapor.
You cannot see water vapor in air.
But it goes up with rising warm air.

What happens when you add heat to a liquid? The liquid changes to gas.

Water Comes out of Air

Remember, when rising air gets high enough,
it gets cool.
And the water vapor in air gets cool too.
Water vapor is a gas.
What happens when a gas gets cool?
Gas changes back to liquid.
When water vapor gets cool,
it changes back to water.

You can see water in air.
Clouds are tiny drops of
water in air.

Water Falls from Air

When the drops of water in clouds get too heavy, they fall from the air.

"Sing unto the Lord with thanksgiving . . . Who covereth the heaven with clouds, who prepareth rain for the earth." Psalm 147:7, 8

Wild Animals

Some animals are wild.
Wild animals do not live with people.

"Behold the fowls of the air: for they sow not, neither do they reap, nor gather into barns; yet your heavenly Father feedeth them." Matthew 6:26

Wild Animals in the Woods

God created some wild animals
to live in the woods.
Bears live in the woods.
What other wild animals live there?
Have you ever seen an animal in the woods?
What animal did you see?

Many times you do not see the animals
in the woods.
How do you know that they are there?
Sometimes you find prints and marks
made by wild animals.
You may even find their homes.

A print is the shape of a foot in snow,
sand, or soft ground.
Look at the animal prints.
Name the animals that made these prints.

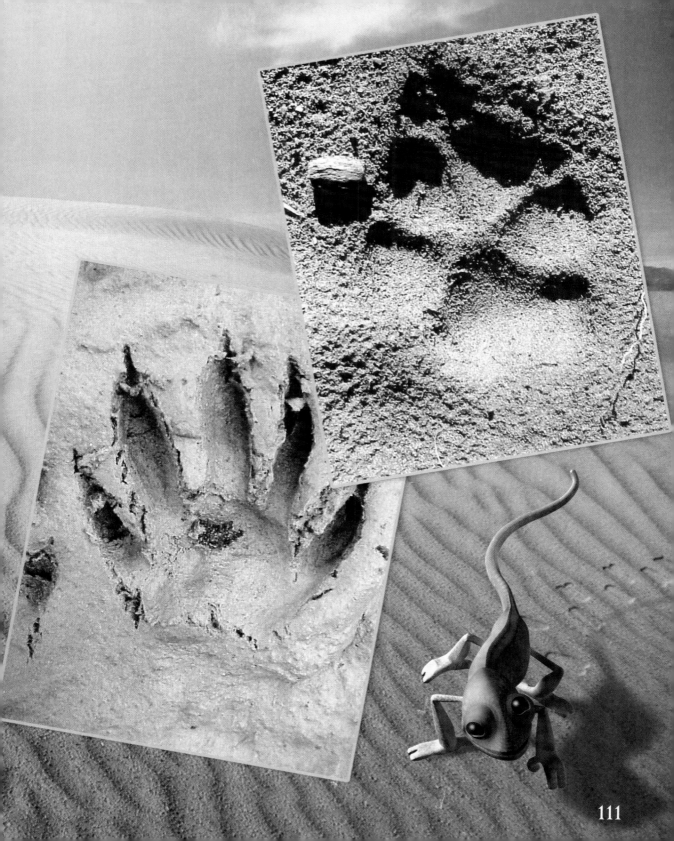

Wild animals sometimes make marks
on trees and other plants.
They also make homes that you can see.

Find where a woodpecker drilled for insects.
Find where a beaver chewed a tree.

Find the animals' homes.

"O Lord, thou preservest man and beast." Psalm 36:6

Wild Animals in Zoos

Some wild animals live in zoos. Elephants, monkeys, and tigers are some wild animals that live in zoos.

Have you been to a zoo? What animals did you see?

Did you see the animal cages
at the zoo?
Cages are places for keeping
animals.

A cage should be easy
and safe to clean.
A cage should be the
right size.
A cage should let you
see the animal well.

Did you see a zookeeper?
A zookeeper is a person
who takes care of zoo animals.

A zookeeper gives the animals food.
A zookeeper gives the animals water.
A zookeeper cleans the cages.

116

Sound

How Is Sound Made?

When you make sound,
something moves back and
forth very fast.
It vibrates.

What is vibrating in these
pictures?

Tell some ways you make
things vibrate.
Did you say hit, rub,
pluck, shake, and blow?

119

How Does Sound Travel?

You cannot see where sound travels. But you can hear where it travels.

Does sound travel up and down?

Does sound travel left
and right?
Does it travel forward
and backward?
Sound travels in all
directions.

Where Sound Travels

1. Get

a piece of paper

2. Make a paper cone.

3. Talk to a friend through the paper cone.
   Can he hear you if he stands
   in front or in back of you,
   on your left or on your right,
   over you or under you?

4. Record what you observed.

Sound travels through all forms of matter.

Sound travels through air.
Air is a gas.
Sound travels through gases.

Sound travels through water.
Water is a liquid.
Sound travels through liquids.

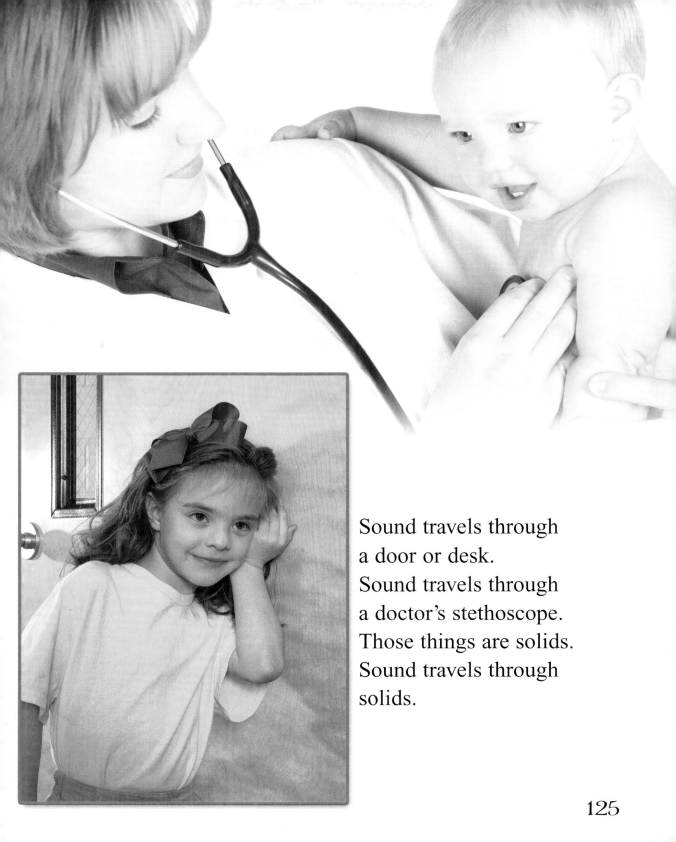

Sound travels through
a door or desk.
Sound travels through
a doctor's stethoscope.
Those things are solids.
Sound travels through
solids.

Finding Out... What Sound Travels Through

1. Get

two shoelaces   two spoons   a jar of water

2. Hit the two spoons together.
   Did sound travel through the air?
   Does sound travel through gases?

3. Hold the spoons underwater.

4. Put your ear against the jar.

5. Hit the spoons together.
   Did sound travel through the water?
   Does sound travel through liquids?

6. Tie one shoelace to one spoon
   and the other shoelace
   to the other spoon.

7. Hold the shoelaces to your ears
   and let the spoons hit each other.
   Did sound travel through the shoelaces?
   Does sound travel through solids?

8. Record what you observed.

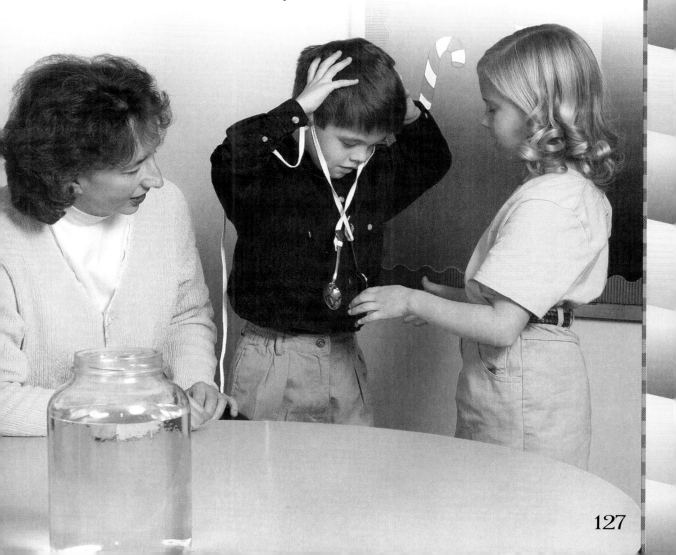

How Is Sound Used?

Some sounds give messages.
What messages do they give?

"There is a sound of abundance of rain." I Kings 18:41

Some sounds give pleasure. Can you name the things that make them?

Flowers, Fruit, and Seeds

CHAPTER TWELVE

Parts for Making New Plants

Many plants grow three parts
to make new plants.
They grow flowers.
They grow fruit.
They grow seeds.

Flowers change to fruit.
Fruit contains seeds.
What grows from seeds?

"*And God said, Let the
earth bring forth . . .
the fruit tree yielding
fruit after his kind,
whose seed is in itself,
upon the earth:
and it was so.*"
Genesis 1:11

Flowers

God made many flowers with colored parts.
The parts are called petals.
The petals of some flowers grow
in groups of three.
The petals of other flowers grow
in groups of four or five.

Look at these flowers.
Find the flowers that
belong in each group.

134

Did you find any flowers
that had too many petals to count?

About Flowers

1. Get

the three pages about
flowers from your *SCIENCE
1 Notebook Packet*

a flower

2. Count the petals as you pull them off.
   How many petals did you count?

3. Find the page with that
   number of petals.

4. Fit one petal on
   each space.
   How many
   groups do your
   petals make?

5. Record what
   you did.

136

Fruit

"And he shall be like a tree
planted by the rivers of water,
that bringeth forth his fruit in his season;
. . . and whatsoever he doeth shall prosper."
                                    Psalm 1:3

God made different kinds of fruit.
Some fruit is juicy.
Other fruit is dry.

Juicy Fruit

Dry Fruit

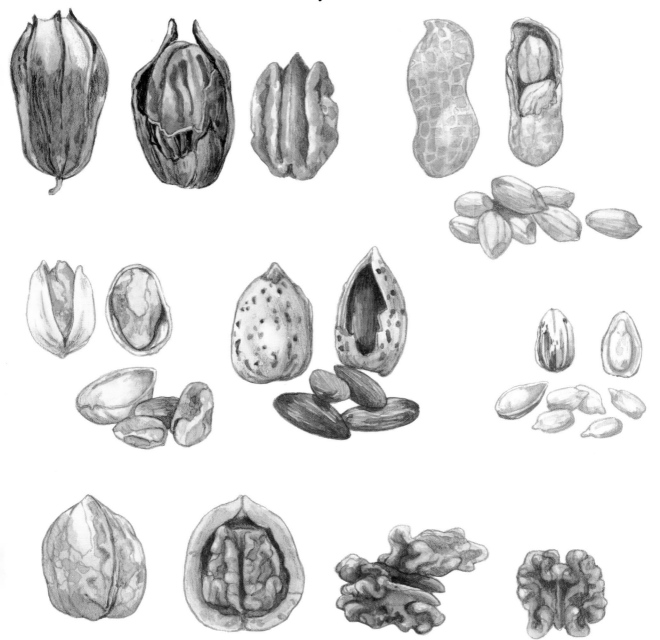

Seeds

God made seeds of many shapes, sizes, and colors.

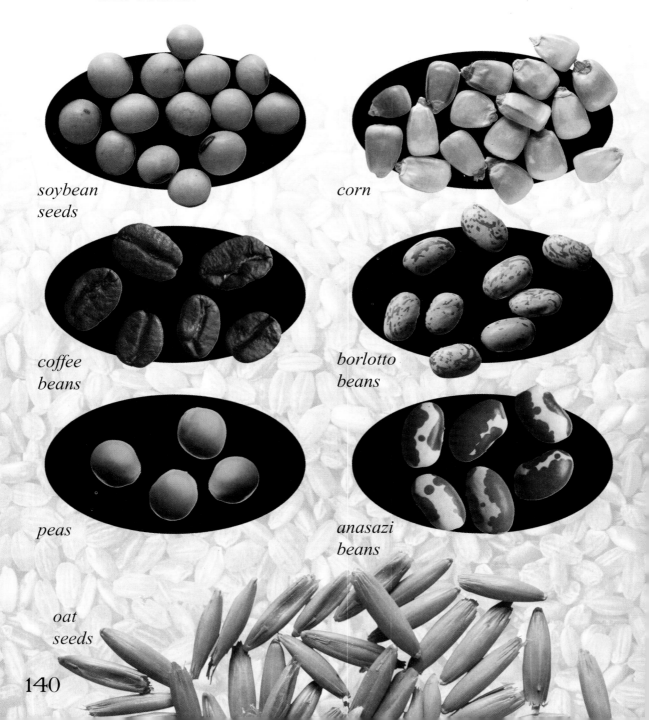

soybean
seeds

corn

coffee
beans

borlotto
beans

peas

anasazi
beans

oat
seeds

Finding Out...

About Fruit and Seeds

1. Get

some fruit

2. Put the fruit into groups.
   Did you get two groups?

3. Open up the fruit.
   What do you see?

4. Record what you observed.

Parts for Eating

Plant parts can be food.
Flowers can be food.
Fruit and seeds can be food too.

Look at the pictures.
Find the pictures of flowers that people eat.
Find the pictures of fruit
and the pictures of seeds.

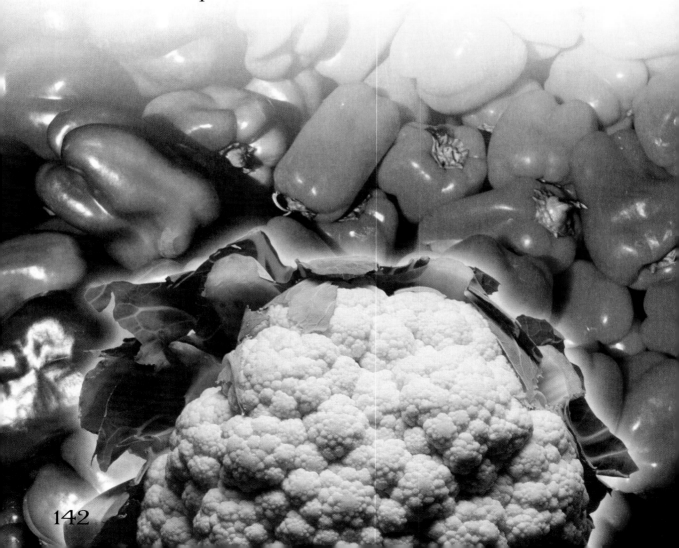

Finding Out...

About Plants People Eat

1. Get

some plants people eat

2. Decide which part you could eat.

3. Record what you did.

fruit　　　**flowers**　　　**see**

144

Talking About Weather

13

You have learned what causes weather.
Now you will learn to describe weather.
Weathermen describe weather.
You will be a weatherman.

The Words of a Weatherman

You can describe the temperature of air.
You can use the numbers on a thermometer.

A weatherman would say,

"The temperature is 90 degrees."

"The temperature is 30 degrees."

"Praise ye the Lord. . . .
he causeth his wind to blow." Psalm 147:1, 18

You can describe the movement of air.
You can use a flag to help you.

A weatherman would say,

"It is calm."

"There is a light breeze."

"There is a gentle breeze."

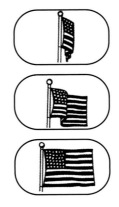

"Praise ye the Lord. . . .
who covereth the heaven with clouds." Psalm 147:1, 8

You can describe how much water
comes out of air.
You can describe how cloudy it is.

A weatherman would say,

"The sky is clear."

"The sky is partly cloudy."

"The sky is cloudy."

You can describe the water
that falls from air.

A weatherman would say,

"It is raining."

 "It is sleeting."

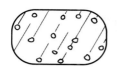 "It is hailing."

"It is snowing."

"For he saith to the snow,
Be thou on the earth; likewise to the small rain."
                                    Job 37:6

The Jobs of a Weatherman

A weatherman observes the weather.
A weatherman records what he observes.

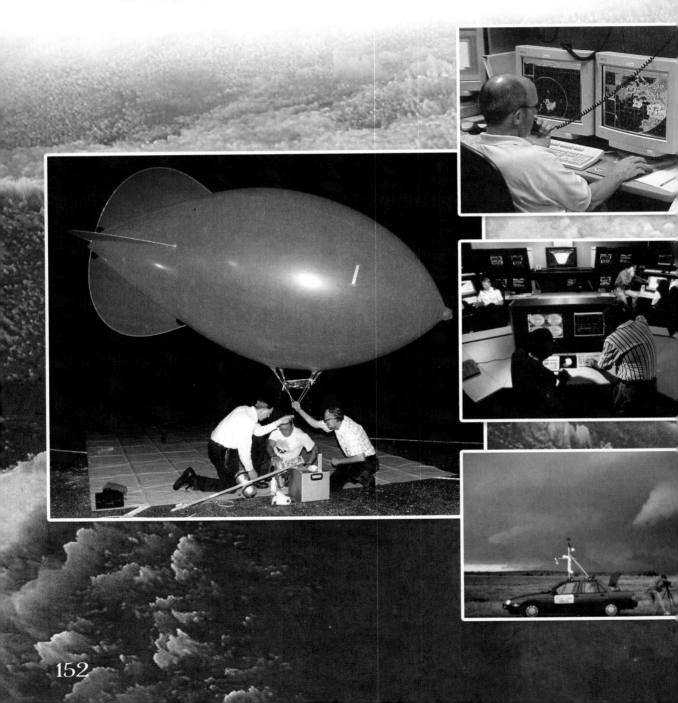

A weatherman reports what he records.

"*Hearken unto this, . . . stand still,
and consider the wondrous works of God.*"

Job 37:14

Good Stewards

A steward takes care of what belongs to someone else.
God has allowed us to live on His wonderful earth.
He gave us tall trees and mountains.
God also gave us big oceans and sandy beaches.
We should take good care of what God has given us.

How can you be a good steward?
You can pick up trash when you see it.
Trash belongs in a trash can, not on the ground.
You should not waste water and food.
You can thank God for all He has given you.

"Moreover it is required in stewards, that a man be found faithful." I Corinthians 4:2

Useful Terms

blow To make noise by forcing air through an instrument: *blow a bugle.*

breeze A light wind.

cage A place for keeping animals in a zoo.

condense To change from a gas to a liquid, usually because heat is removed.

crown The top part of a tooth.

cycle A circular process; a repeated series of events, such as the water cycle or the seasons.

floss Strong thread, such as that used for embroidery or in cleaning teeth.

force A push or pull.

freeze To change from a liquid to a solid when heat is removed.

friction Resistance caused by rubbing. A force that slows or stops the motion of two things touching each other.

gas A form of matter that takes the shape of its container and expands to fill it.

gravity The force that draws objects together; the force that gives people and objects on the earth weight and keeps them from flying off into space.

hit To strike.

juicy Having much juice.

leaf The thin, flat, green part of a plant that grows from the stem and makes food for the plant.

liquid A form of matter that has a definite volume but takes the shape of its container.

magnetic Attracting or attracted to iron.

matter Anything that takes up space and can be weighed.

mechanical Of or using machines or tools.

melt To change from a solid to a liquid when heat is added.

moon The natural satellite that orbits the earth and lights it by night.

neck The part of a tooth at the gums, between the crown and the root.

petal The colored outer part of a flower that gives it shape.

plant A living thing that creates its own food and is not an animal.

pluck To remove by pulling out; pick.

rise To move upward.

root The part of a plant that grows into the soil and absorbs water and nutrients for the plant; the part of a tooth that is in the bone.

science The study of God's creation. All knowledge gained through observing the physical universe.

seed The kernel of a flowering plant from which a new plant grows. A seed contains all the information necessary to grow a new plant.

senses The abilities by which a living thing perceives the world around it. Human beings have five senses: sight, hearing, smell, taste, and touch.

siren A device that makes a loud noise for a warning.

solid A form of matter that keeps its shape and volume.

sound Vibration that the ear hears.

stem The part of a plant that carries water from the roots to the leaves and food from the leaves to the roots.

sun The star that the earth revolves around. On the earth, we see the sun come up in the east and go down in the west.

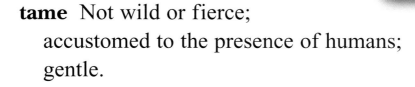

tame Not wild or fierce; accustomed to the presence of humans; gentle.

temperature The amount of heat; how hot or cold something is.

thermometer A device for measuring temperature. Temperature change can be described with the numbers on a thermometer.

vaporize To turn into a vapor or gas.

vibrate To move (or cause to move) rapidly back and forth.

warning An indication that danger is coming.

weather The condition of the atmosphere at a certain time in a certain place. Rain and snow are examples of weather.

weatherman A person who observes, records, and reports the weather.

wild Not tame; living apart from human control or care.

wind Moving air.

zookeeper A person who takes care of zoo animals.

Index

Illustration Credits

Matthew Bjerk pp. 8 (bottom right), 11 (bottom right), 15 (bottom right), 20 (bottom left), 36 (top right), 43 (bottom right), 46 (bottom right), 53 (bottom left), 64 (top right), 81 (bottom left), 95 (middle right), 100 (bottom left), 106 (top right), 111 (bottom right), 119 (bottom left), 136 (bottom right), 153 (bottom right)

Paula Cheadle pp. 38, 77

Michael Cory Godbey p. 69, 156-57

James Hargis pp. 16-17, 22-23, 40-41, 103

Deborah King pp. 1, 13, 18 (top), 9 (top), 25, 29 (top), 37 (top), 45 (top), 48 (top), 49, 54 (top), 62 (top), 63, 72 (top), 73, 82 (top), 83, 92 (top), 97, 102 (top), 107, 117, 122 (top), 126 (top), 131, 136 (top), 141 (top), 144 (top), 145

Lynda Slattery pp. 148-151 (small)

The following artists are represented by Wilkinson Studios, LLC:

Robin Brickman p. 42

Phyllis Pollema Cahill pp. 86-87, 94

Chi Chung pp. 150-51 (large)

Mike Dammer p. 115 (bottom right)

Bob Masheris pp. 75, 146

Drew Rose pp. 33, 76

Kate Sweeney pp. 84, 87 (bottom), 89, 90

Nicole Wong pp. 24, 108

Photograph Credits

The following agencies and individuals have furnished materials to meet the photographic needs of this textbook. We wish to express our gratitude to them for their important contribution.

AbleStock
Suzanne Altizer
Amtrak
© 2003 www.arttoday.com
BJU Press Files
Kim A. Cabrera
George R. Collins
Corbis
Tim Davis
Eastman Chemicals
Kenneth Frederick

Getty Images
Chris Hartzler
Bill Landis
Lick Observatory
NASA
National Oceanic and Atmospheric Administration
National Park Service
National Peach Council
W.R. Okie
Park Seed Company

Susan Perry
Pewag, Inc.
Riverbanks Zoological Park
Wendy Searles
Unusual Films
United States Department of Agriculture
WSPA-TV
Zion National Park

Cover

Digital Vision

Front matter

Unusual Films iii; PhotoLink/Getty Images iv (middle); Siede Preis/Getty Images iv (bottom), iv-v (middle), v (top right); Robert Glusic/Getty Images iv (background); L. Hobbs/PhotoLink/Getty Images iv-v (background top); Jeremy Woodhouse/Getty Images iv-v (background bottom); Riverbanks Zoological Park v (top left); StockTreck/Getty Images v (middle)

Chapter 1

PhotoDisc/Getty Images 2 (left); Corbis 2 (all others); Don Tremain/Getty Images 3 (top); C Squared Studios/Getty Images 3 (bottom), 4 (left, middle, bottom), 5 (left), 6 (left, top, bottom); PhotoLink/Getty Images 4 (top), 7 (background), 11 (top), 12 (top left); Unusual Films 5 (top right, bottom), 9, 12 (middle left); Nancy R. Cohen/Getty Images 6 (background); CMCD/Getty Images 7 (bottom left, top), 8 (middle), 11 (middle); Siede Preis/Getty Images 7 (bottom right), 10 (background), 10-11; Susan Perry 8 (bottom); National Honey Board (top); Allen Rosenberg/Cole Group/Getty Images 10 (middle); Chris Hartzler 12 (bottom left); Edmond Von Hoorick/Getty Images 12 (background); AbleStock 12 (bottom right)

Chapter 2

NASA 14 (top right), 15 (top left), 21 (second moon); PhotoLink/Getty Images 14 (others); Susan Perry 18 (both); StockTrek/Getty Images 19 (bottom); PhotoLink/Getty Images 19 (inset); Lick Observatory, University of California 20 (all), 21 (all other moons); Eastman Chemicals Division 21 (bottom)

Chapter 3

PhotoLink/Getty Images 26 (both); EyeWire/Getty Images 27 (background); Emanuele Taroni/Getty Images 27 (inset); Chris Hartzler 28; Unusual Films 29, 32, 35 (bottom), 36 (others); Amtrak 30 (top); © 2003 www.arttoday.com 30 (bottom); Susan Perry 31 (left), 34 (top, bottom), 35 (top), 36 (left); Wendy Searles 31 (right); Pewag, Inc. 34 (middle)

Chapter 4

Suzanne Altizer 43 (left); Kenneth Frederick 43 (right); Corbis 43 (background), 44 (background); C Squared Studios/Getty Images 44 (bottom left), 46 (both), 47 (all); Siede Preis/ Getty Images 44 (others); Unusual Films 45, 48; C McIntyre/ PhotoLink/Getty Images 46-47 (background)

Chapter 5

Unusual Films 50-51 (both), 52 (both), 53 (both), 54, 55, 62; C Squared Studios/Getty Images 56 (others), 57 (top), 60 (left); Bruce Heinemann/Getty Images 56 (background); Siede Preis/Getty Images 57 (bottom); John Wang/Getty Images 57 (background); PhotoLink/Getty Images 58 (background); Geostock/Getty Images 58 (inset); D. Normark/Getty Images 59 (background); Nancy R. Cohen/Getty Images 59 (inset); Mark Downey/Getty Images 60 (left); MaryBeth Thielhelm/Getty Images 60-61 (background); PhotoLink/Getty Images 61 (top); Corbis 61 (bottom)

Chapter 6

CMCD/Getty Images 64 (left); Corbis 64 (right), 66 (top right, bottom right), 65 (bottom right), 68 (bottom, middle right); C Squared Studios/Getty Images 65 (bottom left); G.K. & Vikki Hart/Getty Images 65 (top left), 68 (middle left, top right); CMCD/Getty Images 66 (left); B. Drake/PhotoLink/ Getty Images 67 (bottom), 70 (bottom); Doug Menuez/Getty Images 67 (bottom); David Buffington/Getty Images 70 (top); S. Solum/Getty Images 71 (top); PhotoLink/Getty Images 71 (bottom); Unusual Films 72

Chapter 7

PhotoLink/Getty Images 74 (top); Nicole Sutton/Life File/Getty Images (bottom); D. Fisher and P. Lyons/Cole Group/Getty Images 78 (left); Kevin Sanchez/Cole Group/ Getty Images 78 (right); Dennis Gray/Cole Group/Getty Images 79 (left); Victor Budnik/Cole Group/Getty Images 79 (right); Unusual Films 82

Chapter 8

Bill Landis 85 (top); Unusual Films 85 (bottom), 92 (both), 96; Corbis 88 (all); Alan and Sandy Carey/Getty Images 91 (top), 93 (top right); AbleStock 91 (bottom left); CMCD/ Getty Images 91 (bottom right); Erin Hogan/Getty Images 93 (top left); PhotoLink/Getty Images 93 (bottom left); Getty Images 93 (bottom right); D. Fischer and P. Lyons/Cole Group/Getty Images 95 (top); C Squared Studios/Getty Images 95 (bottom left); Victor Budnik/Cole Group/Getty Images 95 (bottom right)

Chapter 9

Lee Cates/Getty Images 98 (top left); Hisham F. Ibrahim/Getty Images 98 (middle left); Corbis 98 (bottom left); Jeremy Woodhouse/Getty Images 98 (background); J. Luke/PhotoLink/Getty Images 99 (left); John Dakers/Life File/Getty Images 99 (right); Corbis 99 (background), 106 (bottom); Unusual Films 100-102; AbleStock 104; L. Hobbs/PhotoLink/Getty Images 105 (background), 106 (background); PhotoLink/Getty Images 105 (others)

Chapter 10

Alan and Sandy Carey/Getty Images 109 (left, right); PhotoLink/Getty Images 109 (background), 113 (bottom, top left); Robert Glusic/Getty Images 110-11 (background), 113 (background); Kim A. Cabrera/www.bear-tracker.com 110 (foreground), 111 (left, right); National Park Service 112 (bottom); CMCD/Getty Images 112 (background, inset); Karl Weatherly/Getty Images 113 (top right); Riverbanks Zoological Park 114 (bottom, left), 115 (bottom); Suzanne Altizer 114 (right); Tim Davis 115 (top); BJU Press Files 115 (background); Susan Perry 116 (all)

Chapter 11

C Squared Studios/Getty Images 118 (bottom left), 123 (bottom left), 130 (bottom right); PhotoLink/Getty Images 118 (top left), 120 (top), 123 (top inset), 130 (top left); Unusual Films 118 (top right, bottom right), 122, 125 (bottom), 126, 127, 128 (bottom right); Nicola Sutton/Life File/Getty Images 119 (top); Emma Lee/Life File/Getty Images 119 (middle); Joyce Landis 120 (middle); Kent Knudson/PhotoLink/Getty Images 120-21 (bottom); Corbis 121 (top), 130 (background); Ryan McVay/Getty Images 121 (middle); CMCD/Getty Images 123 (bottom inset); Geostock/Getty Images 123 (background); T. O'Keefe/PhotoLink/Getty Images 124; AbleStock 125 (top), 129 (background); Alan and Sandy Carey/Getty Images 128 (top right); C. Sherburne/PhotoLink/Getty Images 128 (background); National Park Service 129 (top left)

Chapter 12

National Peach Council 132 (top right, bottom right), 133 (top left); W.R. Okie, USDA-ARS 132 (left), 133 (right); Siede Preis/Getty Images 132-33, 140 (top left, top right); Tim Davis 133 (bottom left), 143 (middle); George R. Collins 134 (top); Park Seed Company 134 (bottom); Jules Frazier/Getty Images 134 (background); Bruce Heinemann/Getty Images 135 (bottom left); Suzanne Altizer 135 (middle), 143 (top); Zion National Park, Utah Photo by Victor Jackson 135 (top left); PhotoLink/Getty Images 135 (top right), 137, 142 (background); Unusual Films 136, 141, 144; C Squared Studios/Getty Images 140 (others), 142 (top, bottom); F. Schussler/PhotoLink/Getty Images 140 (background), 143 (background); John A. Rizzo/Getty Images 143 (bottom)

Chapter 13

Patrick Clark/Getty Images 147 (top); Corbis 147 (bottom); PhotoLink/Getty Images 147; J. Luke/PhotoLink/Getty Images 149; StockTrek/Getty Images 152-3; NOAA 152 (all); WSPA-TV (153)

Backmatter

Corbis 159; Siede Preis/Getty Images 160; PhotoLink/Getty Images 161; D. Falconer/PhotoLink/Getty Images 162; Spike Mafford/Getty Images 163

 **Science 1** Start your student on the path of scientific inquiry with an introduction to the senses, heat, sound, animals, and heavenly bodies—presenting God as Creator of all things.

 **Science 2** Present God's earth and His creation clearly as your student studies bones, plants, the shape and movement of the earth, natural forces, and shorelines.

 **Science 3** Direct your student's natural curiosity by helping him describe what God has created. Through studies of classification of animals, the solar system, skin, photosynthesis, birds, mass, and weight, your student will increase his knowledge of the world God made.